When Can I?

written by Thomas Sanders
illustrated by Gregg Thorkelson

BROADMAN
&HOLMAN
PUBLISHERS

NASHVILLE, TENNESSEE

This book is dedicated to my children, Katie, Jayne Claire, and Kyle

Text copyright © 2001 by Thomas Sanders

Illustration copyright © 2001 by Broadman & Holman Publishers

Published in 2001 by Broadman & Holman Publishers, Nashville, Tennessee

Scriptures taken from the King James Version

Cover design and layout by Ernie Hickman.

Library of Congress Cataloging-in-Publication Data

Sanders, Thomas, 1965-
    When can I? : questions preschoolers ask in their first steps toward faith / by Thomas Sanders ; illustrations by Gregg Thorkelson.
    p. cm.
    ISBN 0-8054-2162-9
    1. Christian education--Home training. 2. Christian education of preschool children. I. Thorkelson, Gregg. II. Title.

BV1590 .S36 2002
248.8'2--dc21

2001043323

ISBN 0-8054-2162-9

1 2 3 4 5   05 04 03 02 01

FOREWORD

by Daryl Eldridge

Our children began to ask questions about Jesus, baptism, and joining the church when they were very young. Like other Christian parents, we wanted our children to come to a saving knowledge of Jesus Christ. Mark and Melinda had heard us talk about our faith and observed us witnessing to young people. They watched friends walk down the aisle, talk to the pastor, and later be baptized. Mark, an experiential learner, wanted to know why he couldn't eat the crackers and drink the juice with us during the Lord's Supper. Our children knew what we valued and it was natural for them to be interested in spiritual things.

I had been to seminary and had been a youth minister for several years before we had children. I had led teenagers and adults to Christ, but had not been present at that holy moment when a young child makes a commitment to accept Jesus. I, like many parents, struggled with knowing how to talk to my children about salvation. How do you explain the cross and the resurrection of our Lord in words they will understand? When are they ready to make a decision for Christ? How do you know they understand what they are doing? I knew the correct theological answers, but it's another thing when your children are asking them.

I learned in my child development courses that children can be easily manipulated by adults whom they trust and from whom they desire approval. Carole and I wanted our children to make a profession of their faith, but we wanted it to be a decision they would always remember and not something they did to please us or as a means to eat and drink the elements of the Lord's Supper. We didn't want them to later question what they had done or feel they had been coerced to make a decision they didn't understand. We wished there had been a book that equipped us to share these wonderful, intimate truths with our children.

When Can I? is an invaluable resource for parents and teachers who desire to share Jesus with children. Let me encourage you to read the book several times in preparation for answering your children's questions. Share the book with other parents. You may want to write dates in the book when your children make spiritual decisions. Save the book as a keepsake for your children to be passed on to them when they become parents. There is no greater legacy you can give your children than your faith. May God grant you wisdom in sharing the precious truth of Jesus with your children.

Daryl and Carole Eldridge have two grown children. Daryl is the Dean of the School of Educational Ministries at Southwestern Baptist Theological Seminary and Carole is on the faculty of the School of Nursing at Tarleton State University.

Introduction

For Parents and Teachers

Guiding children to take those first steps toward faith can be the most rewarding opportunity of life for both parents and teachers. The journey toward faith is filled with teachable moments where influential adults and peers answer questions, teach biblical truths, model Christian values, and share personal testimonies that further the child's understanding. Each of these experiences helps prepare him for spiritual conversion. Parents and teachers who have growing relationships with Jesus should create an environment for a child to be introduced to Jesus from the first days of life. As the child grows and matures, his knowledge of Jesus will grow. By laying these foundations for spiritual conversion, teachers and parents become partners with the Holy Spirit as He prepares and calls the child to accept Jesus as Savior.

Jesus as Friend

From the first days of life, a child should begin to associate the name Jesus with positive feelings. During the preschool years, the child needs to associate Jesus with the Bible, church, family, and self. The goal is to lead each preschooler to understand that Jesus is a friend who loves him.

In the younger preschool years, a child can understand that Jesus was a special baby. As a boy, Jesus had a family and went to church. Jesus grew to be a man. Jesus helped people because He loved them. Jesus loves all people and wants people to love Him.

In the middle preschool years, a child begins hearing Bible stories that emphasize Jesus as God's Son. God sent Jesus to the earth. Jesus studied and learned. Jesus did things that people cannot do. Jesus wants people to love and help each other.

For kindergarten-age children, the concepts are enhanced in content and meaning. Jesus is God's one and only Son. Jesus performed miracles and healed the sick. Children can grow like Jesus—in mind, body, and their relationships with God and others. People should follow the example, teachings, and commandments of Jesus. Jesus died on the cross. God made Jesus alive again. Jesus is in heaven.

Jesus as Savior

As a child matures from the preschool years through the elementary years, he moves from the stage of knowing Jesus as friend to an increasing understanding of Jesus as Savior. For a child, becoming a Christian happens both in "bits and pieces" over the years and in one "Big Event." Parents and teachers work with the Holy Spirit in the "bits and pieces" process. They lay the foundations that introduce the child to Jesus as a friend. Then the Holy Spirit in the "Big Event" calls the child to accept Jesus as Savior. Part of the Holy Spirit's role is to reveal to the child his separateness from God because of personal sin. In other words, a child must realize that he is lost before he can be saved. All of this requires time and patience. When a child begins to ask questions, it may only signal the early stages of acquiring more information. Both the child and the Holy Spirit should be in the driver's seat setting the pace and course for discussion. The "Big Event" occurs at different ages for individual children since each child is unique in his relationship with God. Helping a child understand the gospel should not be just a presentation of facts but rather a dialogue that takes time and involves parents, teachers, and ministers. Here are some simple statements to consider.

The child must understand:

…Who is Jesus?

…Why did Jesus come to earth?

…What did Jesus do?

…Why should I become a Christian?

…How can I accept Jesus as my Savior?

The critical aspect of conversion is a life change. Second Corinthians 5:17 reminds us that to be in Christ involves change. This fact is true for children as well. There is no separate gospel for children. There is one gospel for all people. Even though a child may not have much noticeable change, there must be change. Adults who counsel children in matters of conversion must remember this. For a child to have the right answers is not enough. The child must be convicted by the Holy Spirit. It is not merely enough to understand sin in relationship to others. The child must understand and be convicted of his broken relationship with God. Parents and teachers must be sensitive to the Holy Spirit's work. Where there is no conviction, there can be no real change and spiritual conversion. Decisions that last a lifetime are decisions based on true conviction and conversion.

This book was written to help parents and teachers know how to guide children on the journey to accepting Jesus as Savior. The book can be used with young children as questions arise along the journey, older children however, may read the entire book at one time if they have questions about Christianity. Children begin asking questions in a sequence often starting with the ordinances of Baptism and the Lord's Supper. Later they move on to questions of Jesus' death and resurrection, then to the ultimate realization of sin and salvation. These stories offer a way to help children understand elements that are essential to becoming a Christian. Each section features a story which is centered on a particular question most children ask about faith and conversion. The first two stories are written on a kindergarten/younger child level. The later two are written for middle and older elementary-age children. Using the later stories with younger children will require more assistance from parents. This book should not be used to educate a child into conversion. That could lead to a decision that lacks the power of conviction and change. Instead, it should become a responsive tool as the child brings up issues and questions to aid in understanding. Each story offers follow-up questions and a section of general helps dealing with that story's particular question.

General Guidance for Answering Questions Children Have About Faith

• Ask follow-up questions. When a child asks a question, often he does not know exactly what to ask. Get clarification before deciding how to answer a question. For example, you might say, "Tell me more about what you are thinking." Or you may ask: "What made you ask that question? Where did you hear about this?" Remember, many times the question a child asks may not be the actual question he is needing an answer for. Young children may not know what to ask or how to ask for information about Christianity. Also, a child may struggle with putting his questions into words that adults can understand. Avoid asking questions that can be answered with "yes" or "no." This can lead to misunderstandings for both the child and the adult.

• Avoid giving more information than a child needs. Adults can be tempted to tell all they know on a subject. When a child asks a question, only answer what the child is asking. If the child wants more information, they will ask more questions.

• Do not jump to conclusions. A child may ask, "Why did Andy get baptized?" This question may be only a request for information, not a request for the gospel presentation. A child incorporates concepts and information over time. Asking questions allows them to gain information, correct misconceptions, and gain new insights.

• Speak in clear terms. Avoid symbolic analogies that may distract from discussion and understanding.

Parents and teachers should be aware that a child may ask questions they are unprepared to answer, and while they are answering the question the child may even lose interest for a short time. Both extremes can be present over time or even in one visit. Always remain sensitive to the child and the Holy Spirit. God bless you as you join children in making those important steps along the journey to responding to God's call for salvation.

Story 1:
"When Can I Get Baptized?"

8

9

"When Can I Get Baptized?"

As Katie walked with her dad and mom from Sunday School to the worship service, she saw her friend Emily going to the balcony. "Dad, let's sit with Emily," Katie suggested.

As they sat down, Emily handed Katie a church bulletin and said, "Look, Brianna's name is in the bulletin."

Brianna was two years older than Katie and they rode bikes together sometimes. "Why is Brianna's name in the bulletin?" Katie asked her dad.

"I think she became a Christian during Vacation Bible School. She is getting baptized today," replied her dad.

Katie had seen people baptized before, but she had never known someone who was getting baptized. At the beginning of the service, Pastor Paul and Brianna entered the baptistry. The pastor told everyone that Brianna had become a Christian after Vacation Bible School and now she was being baptized. He carefully lowered Brianna back into the water and then raised her up again. The pastor gently wiped the water from Brianna's face. Brianna smiled at him. Katie looked at the people in the church. They were all smiling at Pastor Paul and Brianna. Everyone seemed so happy for Brianna.

Katie tugged on her dad's coat. "Dad, why did Brianna get baptized?"

Her dad leaned down and whispered, "We can talk about it when we get home. I promise." Katie waited patiently.

In the car Katie buckled her seat belt and asked, "Can we talk about Brianna getting baptized?"

"Sure, what was your question?" Dad replied. Katie told her dad that she did not understand what happened. Dad told her that they could look in the Bible for answers.

At home, they read the Bible story about the man from Ethiopia. The man went to Jerusalem to find out more about God. As the man left Jerusalem, he began to read from a Bible scroll. He did not understand what he was reading. God sent a Christian named Philip to help the man from Ethiopia. Philip explained the Bible scroll was telling about Jesus, God's Son. Philip told the man about Jesus and what He did. The Ethiopian man believed what Philip had said and became a

Christian. The Ethiopian man told Philip he would like to be baptized.

"What does baptism mean?" asked Katie

Katie's dad thought for a few minutes before he answered. "When a person becomes a Christian, baptism is the way she shows that she has become a Christian. This also shows that she wants to be a member of the church. Baptism also is an important way people show that they want to be like Jesus for the rest of their lives. When someone is baptized, she is showing that she is doing what God wants her to do. Sometimes before being baptized, children attend a class that teaches them more about becoming a Christian."

"Is the water magic?" asked Katie.

"No," said Dad. "When you get baptized, nothing magical happens. You just get wet. It's water just like the water we have at home."

The next day after school Katie and her dad went to visit Pastor Paul. Together they went to look at the baptistry. This time it was empty, except for a little water on the floor. Katie's tennis shoes squeaked as she walked down the steps into the baptistry. Katie looked out into the empty worship center. She remembered Brianna and how happy everyone was last Sunday. Katie told Pastor Paul about her talk with her dad. Pastor Paul told Katie that baptism is very important, but a person must first become a Christian. He told her it was an important decision. He also said that God would let her know when it was the right time. Pastor Paul told her that he would look forward to talking with her again.

"Dad, one day I want to become a Christian and be baptized," said Katie.

Katie's dad responded, "I'm glad you are asking these questions. I'm glad that we have the Bible and people like Pastor Paul to help us know about baptism. God loves you, Katie, and He has a special plan for you. Your mom and I want to help you as you learn more about Jesus."

15

Follow-up Questions for Parents and Teachers

Why do people get baptized?

What does baptism mean?

What happens when a person gets baptized?

Does a person have to get baptized to be a Christian?

Guidance for Parents and Teachers

Baptism is a public ceremony; it catches the attention of most children, especially if they see other children being baptized. This may be the reason that the first question a child asks about faith is related to baptism. Helping children understand this important symbol of Christianity is essential to their over-all spiritual development. While most adult Christians have a clear understanding of the relationship between baptism and becoming a Christian, our language is sometimes confusing. Frequently, the terms "baptism" and "becoming a Christian" are used interchangeably, which leads to many misconceptions for children. Here are some guidelines in helping children understand baptism.

• Always make distinctions between baptism and becoming a Christian.

• Point out that becoming a Christian comes first and then baptism follows because it is a way of showing they have become a Christian.

• Avoid emphasizing the emotional side of the baptism experience. Children respond in different ways during the actual baptism. Beware of setting false expectations. Also, keep in mind that public recognition should not become a motivating factor for making a decision.

• Plan a trip to the baptistry when it is not in use.

• Use simple wording. Rather than using the phrase "Accepting Jesus into your heart," say the words "Becoming a Christian."

Other images of baptism—the symbol of the death, burial, and resurrection of Jesus and the death of the old life and beginning of a new life—can be explained as the child grows in her understanding of becoming a Christian and the ordinance of baptism. Explain that the act of going into the water is a symbol of Jesus' death and burial and being raised up out of the water is a symbol of Jesus' resurrection.

Always begin with the simple truths and build toward the more complex images.

Story 2:
"When Can I Take The Lord's Supper?"

18

"When Can I Take The Lord's Supper?"

Zip, buckle, clip went the seat belt as Claire sat down in the car. She and her family were traveling to church. Mom reminded them that during the regular worship service today there would be a special service called the Lord's Supper. "Claire, do you remember seeing the Lord's Supper?" asked Mom.

"Is that when the preacher gives out little cups of juice and crackers?" replied Claire.

"Yes, it's a time for us to remember all the things Jesus did for us. It is important for us to listen carefully during this part of the worship service," continued Mom.

At the front of the sanctuary, Claire noticed a big table covered with a white cloth. She remembered that this cloth was covering the juice and crackers for the Lord's Supper. The pastor and some other church helpers removed the cloth. The pastor began to tell a Bible story about the Lord's Supper. The pastor said, "Jesus wanted to have a special meal with His disciples in an upstairs room in Jerusalem. At the end of the meal, Jesus told His disciples that He would soon die. They were very sad to hear this. They could hardly believe that Jesus would die and that they would have to live without Him. Jesus told them this special meal would be an important way to remember Him and remind them how much He loved them."

The pastor picked up one of the crackers. "This bread is like the bread they used in Bible times. The people in Bible times would eat this flat bread to remember a time when God had protected His people in Egypt. Jesus chose to use this bread because it would remind the disciples that God would take care of them. It also would remind them that Jesus gave His body and died for them, so that they could live for God here on earth and one day live with Him in heaven."

Claire watched as the pastor and deacons passed plates of the flat bread to people in the church. Claire watched as her mom and dad each took a small piece of bread. They prayed and slowly ate the bread. Claire wondered what her parents were thinking and what the bread tasted like.

Then the pastor took a cup. He said that people in Bible times had two kinds of drinks—water and a drink made from grapes. Water was used every day, but this kind of grape juice was used for special meals. He told the people that each time the disciples would drink this juice

they would remember how much it hurt Jesus to have bled and died so that they could live with God in heaven.

Claire was beginning to feel sad as she thought about Jesus dying. But as she watched people around the church drink from the small cups, she saw that they were happy.

At the end of the service, the pastor said something that really made Claire feel better. He told the people to remember that Jesus had not only died, but that He is alive in heaven. He said, "Every time you drink this juice and eat this bread, remember that God sent Jesus for us all. Remember that God sent Jesus because He loved us." The pastor then had the people in the church quote John 3:16: "For God so loved the world, that he gave his only begotten Son, that whosoever believeth in him should not perish, but have everlasting life."

As they drove home that day, Claire asked her mom, "When can I take some of the bread and grape juice in the Lord's Supper?"

"Claire, one day when you become a Christian, the Lord's Supper will be more important to you," answered her mother. "When a person becomes a Christian, they begin to understand all that the bread and the grape juice mean. Just like baptism, the Lord's Supper is an important way to show that you love Jesus after you become a Christian."

"Mom, I do love Jesus now," replied Claire.

"Yes, you do and each time you see the Lord's Supper you can show Jesus you love Him by drawing a picture about it, writing a story about your thoughts, or saying a prayer to thank God for sending Jesus. We have many ways to show our love for Jesus," said Mom. "Remember Claire, anytime you have questions, we'll talk about them."

Follow-up Questions for Parents and Teachers

Why do you think Jesus decided to have this special supper?

What is the most important thing to remember about the Lord's Supper?

What are some things you can do during the Lord's Supper to remember Jesus?

Guidance for Parents and Teachers

The Lord's Supper (communion) is a wonderful picture that paints an image of the sacrifice of Jesus for our sins. It includes the senses of taste, sound, sight, smell, and touch—everything a child would want—but it is a complex picture for concrete thinkers. Think about words or phrases spoken at the Lord's Supper. "This is my body ... take and eat it. This is my blood ... drink it." Can these words be confusing? Here are some suggestions for making the Lord's Supper inclusive of and helpful to a young child.

• Prepare the child for the experience. It is essential to prepare older preschoolers and younger children for the first observation of the Lord's Supper.

• Keep it simple. Begin with the basic facts. The Lord's

Supper is a time when we remember all the things that Jesus did for us, and we say "thank you" to God. As the child grows, build on the basic truths, adding specific elements of the Lord's Supper. This may take time. Allow the child and the Holy Spirit to guide you.

• Help the child feel included. Give specific activities to do during the Lord's Supper, such as listening for key words, drawing a picture, or writing a prayer. Encourage the child to share it with the pastor or a minister after the service. Your pastor may want to speak to the children during the service to affirm their participation at some level. In smaller congregations where the pastor administers the elements to each person, he may want to speak a prayer or blessing quietly to each child who has not made a decision.

The feeling of exclusion can lead a child to voice an interest in becoming a Christian that may be only a temporary response to the situation. Take all interest shown by the child seriously, but remember that a child must make a decision because he senses conviction and separateness from God, not because he feels excluded from a church ordinance. Salvation must be the work of the Holy Spirit.

Note: If you are in a situation where your child has already participated in the Lord's Supper but is not a Christian, be sure to find a way to make his first Lord's Supper experience, after he has become a Christian, a very special occasion.

"Why Did Jesus Come ?"

In a flash the light was on in Kyle's room. Kyle squinted in the bright light. "This can't be a school day. I am at Mimi's and Pawpaw John's for spring break. Why is Mimi coming into my room so early?" he thought. Then Kyle mumbled, "It's too early," as he pulled the pillow over his head.

"Kyle, today is Easter and you know we are going to the sunrise service," explained Mimi.

"But Mimi, I don't think even Jesus is up this early," exclaimed Kyle. He dressed slowly with Mimi helping him tuck in his shirt.

As the family drove to church, Kyle noticed that it was still dark outside. His grandparents went to a church on a hill with lots of oak trees. Getting out of the truck, Kyle saw one of his cousins, Sydney. She looked just as sleepy as Kyle did. Instead of meeting inside the church, they met behind the church in a clearing where chairs had been placed. It was just about dawn.

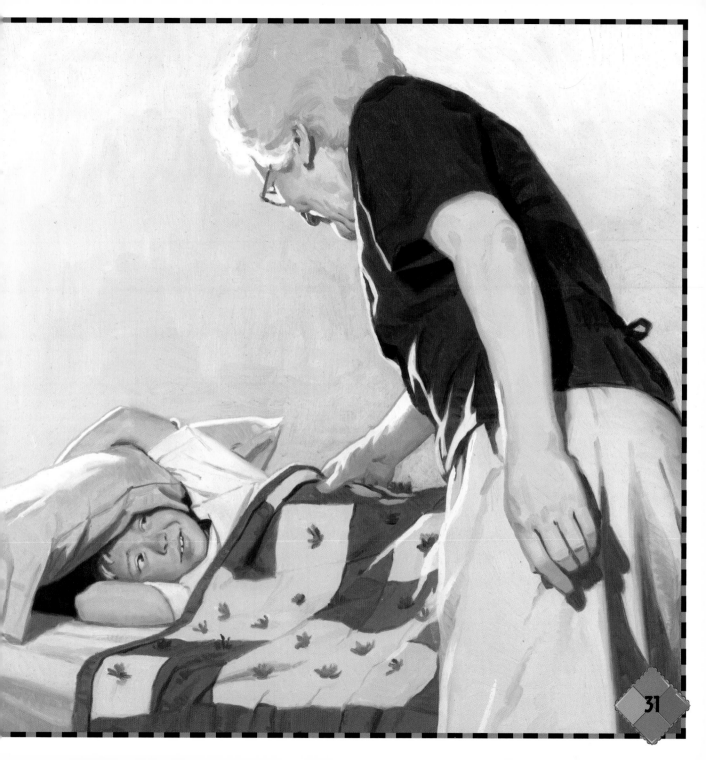

Everyone sang songs and prayed just like any church service, except there was barely enough light to see. Kyle expected the preacher to speak, but instead a woman dressed in Bible clothes moved to the front. She looked very happy. By this time, Kyle could see her face clearly because the sun was beginning to shine through the tall oak trees. The woman began to tell her story. She said that she was Mary Magdalene. "As we walked toward the tomb that morning, it was just about sunrise. We cried as we walked. We could not believe that our Jesus had died on a cross. When we arrived at the grave, we were frightened by an angel dressed in bright clothing. He was sitting on the large stone that had been rolled away from the grave. He told us the greatest news. He said that Jesus was alive! We could not believe it. My sadness could now become happiness. When we heard the news, we ran as fast as we could to tell the disciples. At that moment, I saw Jesus. I ran to him and hugged him. I was so happy to see Him. He told me to go tell His disciples that He would join them soon."

As the woman dressed as Mary Magdalene left the service, the sun was now shining bright outside. The dogwood trees were filled with their white blooms. Kyle now understood why his grandparents wanted to get up early and go to church on Easter. He had never thought about what it meant for Jesus to die and live again.

Sydney joined Kyle and his grandparents for breakfast. Mimi asked the

children what they liked about the sunrise service. Sydney said it was okay, but she wished it was a noontime service. "What about you, Kyle?" asked Mimi.

Kyle told them he liked hearing the story early in the morning, just like when the people that very first Easter heard that Jesus was alive. But he had a question. "I don't understand why Jesus had to die?" As they talked around the breakfast table, Mimi reminded them that Jesus came for one reason. He came to make a way for people to have a relationship with God and live forever with Him. Mimi told the children that God gave people a choice—to sin or to obey Him.

"Do you know what sin is?" asked Mimi.

"I do," said Sydney. "It is when people do bad things."

"That is part of it, Sydney. We sin anytime that we choose to do things our way instead of God's way. All people sin. Sin separates us from God. God loved people so much that He wanted them back with Him. He wants to have a relationship with each person. God made all people. He is very sad when we choose to do things our way instead of His way. The only way for people like you and me to come back to God is for someone who never sinned to die for us. Someone had to be punished for our sins. God sent His only Son to die for us. Jesus never sinned, but He had to die for our sins so that we would not be separated from God. Jesus came to the earth to teach us about God and His love and to provide a way for us to be with God forever."

"That really makes Easter mean even more," said Kyle. "It means not only that Jesus is alive, but that He died so that we could live better lives and live with God forever."

Mimi patted Kyle's hand and said, "You are right, Kyle. Knowing Jesus and loving God makes life wonderful."

Follow-up Questions for Parents and Teachers

Do you know what Easter is really about?

Who was Jesus?

Why did God send Jesus?

Why did Jesus have to die?

Guidance for Parents and Teachers

The Bible would just be another ancient book, except for the story of the birth, life, death, and resurrection of Jesus. Easter tells the story about God, who was unwilling to let His people die without Him. For children, the story unfolds and reveals more and more with each year of growth and awareness. When you tell the story of Easter to children, keep the following things in mind.

• Consider the age of the child. Tell the story in a way that creates an image of hope, not despair. For older preschoolers and younger children, Easter comes just a few months after Baby Jesus was born at Christmas. It may be too difficult for them to understand a story about His adulthood. Work toward the Easter story by looking at Jesus' childhood and adult life in the days and weeks leading up to Easter.

• Follow the Bible. Use the text of the Bible as a guide, rather than adding descriptions that may sidetrack the child. Allow younger children to create pictures in their minds rather than using illustrations that may alarm them. Remember to focus on the resurrection. The story does not end with death. Too many extra biblical descriptions could prevent the child from getting to the resurrection.

• Treat the story as foundational to faith. Children need to hear the Easter story over time to begin to understand its full impact. The Holy Spirit will build upon each telling of the story, leading the child to a new level of understanding. Remember that hearing the facts of the story is not enough for a child to respond to the gospel. The Holy Spirit must convict the child. He must know that he is lost before he can be saved. This process involves a mysterious moving of God that is unique to each person.

• Avoid mixing a fantasy about Easter (such as the "Easter bunny") with the true story of the resurrection. Older preschoolers and younger children have a difficult time separating fact and fiction. Separate the fantasy of Easter traditions from the fact of the faith story of the resurrection. The Bible is the best tool to tell the story.

Share the joy of Easter in ways boys and girls can understand the gift of God to us all.

39

"How Can I Become A Christian ?"

"Just as I Am" was the hymn the people were singing in church. Peter stood with his parents and his little brother Jared, but he was not singing. He was thinking. Peter could feel something different happening. He seemed to be just standing there holding on to the back of the church pew. Today Peter listened closely as the pastor talked about how to become a Christian. This was not the first time Peter thought about it, but this time it seemed very important. Peter wondered if he should walk to the front of the church during the invitation, but he was a little afraid of walking in front of everyone.

About that time, his dad said, "Peter, is everything okay?"

"I don't know. I think I need to walk to the front and talk with Mr. Tommy," replied Peter. Mr. Tommy was the Children's Minister at Peter's church. He stood with the pastor at the front of the church to help people who walked forward during the invitation.

Peter's dad leaned over and whispered, "I think you should go talk with Mr. Tommy, if you want to. I'm sure he would like to help you."

Peter stepped out of the pew and walked forward. Mr. Tommy met Peter at the front of the church. "Peter, tell me why you came forward today."

"I want to talk to you about becoming a Christian," Peter explained.

"Let's take a moment and pray that God will help us know what to do. Then after the service we can visit with your parents about this. Is that okay?" Peter nodded yes. Mr. Tommy prayed with Peter and they stood together until the service was over. At the end of the service, Mr. Tommy and Peter went to find his family. "Mr. Holmes, can you and I go to my office to visit with Peter for a few minutes?" asked Mr. Tommy.

As they sat in the office, Mr. Tommy asked Peter to tell him how long he had been thinking about becoming a Christian. Peter told him he had been thinking about it for several months. Mr. Tommy told Peter that becoming a Christian is the most important thing that can happen to a person.

"I invited your dad to listen to our conversation. Parents are very important, and I want your dad to sit and listen to us talk today. Do you know when your dad became a Christian?" asked Mr. Tommy.

"Yes, I think it was during Vacation Bible School when he was nine or ten," answered Peter. Peter's dad smiled and shook his head yes.

Mr. Tommy explained that becoming a Christian happens at different times for people. He explained that he began asking questions when he was eight but did not become a Christian until he was 14. Mr. Tommy asked Peter to tell him why he wanted to become a Christian. Peter thought for a moment and then began to tell about his conversations with his parents and his Sunday School teacher Miss Louise. Peter told how he felt sorry for the things he had done wrong and the times he had disappointed God.

"Peter, you mentioned the times that you had disappointed God. Do you know what it is called when you choose to do things that disappoint God?" asked Mr. Tommy.

"Yes, it is called sin," replied Peter.

"You are right. It is called sin. Sin separates us from God. That is the reason that Jesus had to die. God wanted to forgive our sins and the only way was for His son to die for us." Mr. Tommy read several Bible passages to Peter. One of the verses was Romans 3:23: "For all have sinned, and come short of the glory of God." Mr. Tommy talked more about why a person must become a Christian.

"Peter, do you know how to become a Christian?" asked Mr. Tommy. Peter told his dad and Mr. Tommy that he thought that he must pray and ask God for forgiveness. Mr. Tommy read some other verses and told Peter that he was correct, but that it did not stop there. He said, "Becoming a Christian begins with asking for forgiveness, but continues with becoming more like Jesus. This is what it means to ask Jesus to be your Savior and Lord. He saves you from your sins and you must choose to obey Him for the rest of your life. There will be times when you sin and you will need to ask for forgiveness, but that does not mean you become a Christian again. It means you are growing in your understanding of what it means to follow Christ."

Mr. Tommy began to tell Peter about the next steps. "Peter, I want you to go home today and think about what we said here. If you feel this is truly what God wants you to do, I want you to tell your mom and dad. Then find a private place in your house and talk to God with your parents. Your parents are the most important people to help you with this decision. Then next Sunday we will share your decision with our church. After that we can talk about baptism and a new Christian's class. Do you have any other questions?"

After talking a little more, Mr. Tommy gave Peter a book to read during the week. Then Mr. Tommy prayed with Peter and his dad. Mr. Tommy told them to call him if they had any other questions.

45

Follow-up Questions for Parents and Teachers

What caused Peter to think about becoming a Christian?

Why do you think Peter wanted to become a Christian?

Why do people need to become Christians?

How do people actually become Christians?

What happens after you become a Christian?

Guidance for Parents and Teachers

There is no decision as life-changing or eternal as the decision to become a Christian. For this reason, children need to be counseled with the greatest care, wisdom, and integrity. Our goal should not be to get a "yes" answer. Our goal is to aid in understanding, as a partner with the Holy Spirit. Parents and teachers, no matter how experienced and well-trained, cannot call a child to salvation, but we can be tools of the Holy Spirit in accordance with God's plan for the child. Parents and teachers often ask, "What are the signs that a child is struggling with becoming a Christian?" Just as children are unique, the signs of conviction are unique.

You must know the personality of the child and deal with each child as an individual.

One of the most common indications that a child is thinking about Christianity is persistent questions about salvation, sin, death, or even hell. The key in knowing how to answer is to let the child set the pace and depth of the responses. Children will come back for more answers if they require more information. Remember to look for the intent of the questions. You may wish to refer back to the introduction of this book.

The Discussion
Below are some hints in talking with the child about salvation.

• *Involve parents* – Parents play an important role in a child's decision. There are situations where parents have no interest or desire to be involved. This represents an opportunity to witness to the parents. A child who lives in a home where faith is not nurtured will have a difficult journey. Our goal should be to give every child a Christian home. If possible, get permission and invite parents to observe your discussion. At the beginning of the session, explain that parents are there to listen, not to talk. If applicable, ask parents to share their personal testimonies.

• *Remain conversational* – Many adults fall into two traps when counseling children about salvation. The first is to make it only a presentation. The second is to make it a question-and-answer test. In reality, the experience should be a dialogue or conversation. The conversation should focus on the child's comments. Therefore, each conversation will be different.

• *Avoid symbolic language or analogies* – A child does not possess truly abstract capabilities until later in adolescence. Speak in simple and concrete terms. Rather than using the phrase "Accepting Jesus into your heart," say the words "Becoming a Christian."

• *Encourage the child to express his own ideas* – Let the conversation be natural and at ease. If the discussion turns to hell or the eternal consequences of sin, deal with it in a factual way, but not in a way that would cause fear.

• *Give time for thought* – Silence can be unbearable, but children need time to think. Open-ended questions require thought. Affirm the child for taking time to think. Smile and wait patiently.

• *Rely on the Bible* – The Bible is really the only resource you need to lead a child to Christ. The actual dialogue should be centered on the Bible. Other tools that are symbolic, such as color-coded cards or beads, can actually confuse a child by immersing them in analogies that hold little or no meaning to a concrete-thinking child.

The Plan
The following plan is simple. It utilizes five simple statements and Scriptures that will help you as you discuss Christianity with young children.   Before you begin remember to (A) Determine the true intent. The first part of any conversation with a child should begin with open-ended questions that allow the child (not the parent) to express his desire. (B) Determine the context. In some cases, children begin to think about becoming a Christian because of a situation or event. A friend may have become a Christian or a child may want to participate in the Lord's Supper. Knowing this information can help you know how to guide the discussion. Begin with simple questions: "How long have you been thinking about becoming a Christian?" "When did you first start thinking about becoming a Christian?"

Model Discussion
1. **God loves you and has a great plan for you**. (Psalm 139:13-16)
Hopefully, a child has been hearing this truth since the first day of life, but there are people all around us who are unaware of this most basic truth.   Begin speaking in warm terms about God. Emphasize these truths: God made the world, God made people, God made you, God wants to have a relationship with people, and God wants to have a relationship

with you. Say, "Tell me one thing that is special about the way God made you."

To transition to the second point you may wish to say, "We know that God loves us and has a great plan for us, but why does a person need to become a Christian?" This question should lead into a discussion of sin.

2. **We have all sinned** (Romans 3:23)
The child must understand his "separateness from God." Sin is best understood as choosing to do things our way instead of God's way. Avoid talking about sin in a way that invades the child's privacy or causes unnecessary guilt. Consider these questions: "What is sin?" "Have you ever sinned?" "What does God think about sin?" "How does sin affect our relationship with God?"

Reinforce the child's understanding by pointing out that all people sin (Romans 3:23).

3. **Even though we choose to sin, God still loves us and offers to forgive us**.
(Romans 5:8)
Ask, "How do you think it makes God feel when we sin?" Continue focusing on the fact that God loves us even though we sin. Say, "God promised that one day a Savior would come to the world. That Savior would not sin and would die for all people. Do you know who that Savior is?"

4. **Jesus died for us**. (John 3:16)
Ask, "Tell me what you know about Jesus?" Talk about John 3:16. Explain, "Because our sins separate us from God, we needed a Savior – someone who would not sin, but do all that God wanted Him to do." Ask, "Do you know why Jesus died?" Say, "God sent His only Son Jesus. Jesus died willingly for our sins so we could be with God forever. That is how much He loved us." Ask, "What happened to Jesus after He died?" Explain that Jesus rose

from the dead so we could have eternal life. We live for Him here on earth, and one day will live with Him in heaven.

5. **You become a Christian by confessing Jesus as your Savior and Lord**.
(Romans 10:9)
Ask, "Do you know how to become a Christian?" State: "The word 'confess' means 'to say something.' You confess that Jesus is your Savior and Lord. First admit you are a sinner. Then you must also 'repent' or turn from sin and say to God that you are sorry for your sins. When you become a Christian, you are saying to God you will go His direction instead of your own. That is what it means when you say Jesus is your Lord."

Review and Follow-up (II Corinthians 5:17)
Encourage the child to tell you in his own words what he understands. If the parents are present they may wish to talk with the child because God has given parents the ultimate responsibility for their children.

The decision—ask the child, "Do you want to become a Christian? Do you want Jesus to be your Lord and Savior?" If the answer is yes, review that the child must pray: **A**dmitting he has sinned and is sorry for his sin. **B**elieving that Jesus is God's Son, and **C**onfessing that Jesus is his Savior and Lord. Encourage the child to pray in his own words.

After the child prays, read Romans 10:13 and remind him this verse is a promise. It means that he has become a Christian. Suggest some special way to remember the occasion such as writing the date in his Bible, beginning a journal, taking a family photo, etc. Encourage the family to have a daily devotional. Also, discuss with him how the church handles the next step for baptism.

Becoming a Christian is the beginning of an exciting journey that doesn't end until we are reunited with Jesus in heaven.